5-16

NATIONAL
GEOGRAPHIC
KiDS

# EVERYTHING
# SPORTS

NATIONAL
GEOGRAPHIC
KiDS

# EVERYTHING SPORTS

**ERIC ZWEIG**

With sports reporter SHALISE MANZA YOUNG

NATIONAL GEOGRAPHIC
WASHINGTON, D.C.

# CONTENTS

College wrestlers compete in the Big Ten Wrestling Championships, a tournament held every year in the United States. Wrestling is a combat sport that has its roots in ancient Greece and Rome.

Volleyball is a team sport widely played in schools and recreation centers, and at sporting events such as the Olympics.

# INTRODUCTION

## A FAMOUS NEWSPAPER

**WRITER ONCE SAID, "SPORTS IS THE TOY** department of life." From baseball to parkour to pole vaulting, there are so many cool sports to play and watch that almost everyone is a fan of something. Sports are exciting for both amateurs and professionals. And they're fun to watch, whether you play the sport or not. Great athletes can sometimes inspire us to do great things, both on and off the field. Sports have also become so much a part of everyday life that they have crept into our speech. If something is easy or obvious, we say it's a "slam dunk!" If you do something that is really impressive, it's a "home run!" Let's face it, sports are all around us and are tons of fun. So, ready, set, and get in gear. It's time to learn EVERYTHING there is to know about sports.

## EXPLORER'S CORNER

**Hi! I'm Shalise Manza Young.**
I am a sports journalist. I have covered tons of sports, from high school to college to professional levels, from basketball to ice hockey to field hockey, and even the first two Summer X Games. I have spent the last nine years covering the NFL's New England Patriots and have been to seven Super Bowl games. I love all sports, and I'm excited to share some of what I know with you in this book. Check out my Explorer's Corners throughout the book to learn more about the fascinating and fun world of sports.

Snowboarding is a fairly new sport, having been developed as a winter activity that combined the skills of surfing, skateboarding, and skiing on a single board. It became an Olympic sport in 1998.

# 1

# SPECTACULAR SPORTS

# WHAT IS A SPORT?

## WHAT IS A SPORT? THE WORD
**"SPORT" MAY HAVE ROOTS IN THE OLD FRENCH WORD *DESPORT*,**
meaning "leisure" or "diversion." It was first used in English about 700 years ago. Back then, the word meant an activity that offered amusement or relaxation, entertainment, and fun. That's still true, but if that's all that sports were, then going to a movie or telling a joke could be a sport. Today when we think of sports, we think of a physical activity that involves skill and competition. There are usually rules to make sure the competition is fair. Sports can be played just for fun, or for a lot of money. Some sports are played by only one or two people at a time, but others can involve a dozen or more athletes playing in teams.

In the game of cricket, a batsman hits the ball with a stroke or shot.

Orienteering is a sport that combines hiking and running with map and navigational skills. Participants use maps and compasses to find their way to the finish of a course.

## MOST POPULAR SPORTS

What makes a sport the most popular? Is it the number of people who play it, or the number of people who call themselves fans? There is no set rule, but when it comes to fans, the most popular sports in the world are:

**SOCCER**—more than 3 billion fans

**CRICKET**—nearly 3 billion fans

**BASKETBALL**—nearly 3 billion fans

**FIELD HOCKEY**—more than 2 billion fans

**TENNIS**—about 1 billion fans

**GAME TIME** TWELVE STRAIGHT STRIKES FOR 300 POINTS IS A PERFECT GAME IN BOWLING.

A rock climber wears a harness attached to ropes to help protect her from falling.

## WHAT ISN'T A SPORT?

Even though they can be competitive and do have rules, board games and video games aren't usually thought of as sports. On the other hand, the International Olympic Committee considers chess to be a sport, and the card game bridge, too. SportAccord is a worldwide organization of sports federations for non-Olympic and Olympic sports. SportAccord defines a sport as:

- including an element of competition;
- not relying only on an element of luck;
- not posing undue health and safety risks; and
- not being harmful to any living creature.

## IN IT TO WIN IT?

Competition is a key part of sports, but sometimes athletes are only competing against themselves or against the elements. Runners who never enter a race might still compete against the clock by trying to beat their own best times. You don't need to compete against other people for an activity to be considered a sport.

TRACK AND FIELD IS A HIGH PARTICIPATION SPORT AROUND THE WORLD, AS MANY PEOPLE ENJOY RUNNING FOR FITNESS.

# By the Numbers

**9.58** seconds is the world record time for the 100-meter sprint, set by Usain Bolt.

**100** runs scored by one batsman in a single inning in cricket is known as a century.

**212.8** miles an hour (342.5 km/h) is the NASCAR speed record set by Bill Elliott in 1987.

**295.27** is the world record point count earned by figure skater Patrick Chan at an event in 2013.

# GO FOR THE GOLD

## IF YOU DON'T KEEP SCORE, HOW DO YOU KNOW
### WHO WINS? THOUGH IT'S RARELY FUN TO LOSE, ONE OF THE THINGS THAT

makes sports great is finding out who's the best at something, whether it's just the best team in a game that day or the best athlete of all time. There are all sorts of prizes and trophies in sports, but you won't see these honors being given out after a game!

### MICHAEL PHELPS

With 18 Olympic gold medals to store along with his 26 World Championship golds, swimmer Michael Phelps practically has his own Fort Knox. Phelps has won 22 Olympic medals in total, and that makes his win record hard to beat.

### GREATEST OLYMPIC MEDAL HAUL

### TALLEST SHOT BLOCKER

Sudan-born Manute Bol's name means "special blessing" in the Dinka language. At 7 feet 7 inches (2.3 m) tall, Bol was among the National Basketball League's tallest players. Using his height to his advantage, he also held the rookie shot-blocking record for the 1985–86 season, and he tied the NBA record for most shots blocked in one game half (11) and one quarter (8).

### GOTCHA COVERED

The only tennis player in history to claim top spot in both singles and doubles for over 200 weeks, Martina Navratilova has been called the greatest tennis player of all time because of her skills and number of wins. Navratilova played singles, doubles, and mixed doubles (males and females playing together), and won 18 Grand Slam singles titles. Grand Slams are the most important annual tennis events.

## ALL-ROUNDER

Mildred Ella "Babe" Didrikson Zaharias was a great all-around athlete. She won gold medals in hurdles and javelin, plus a silver in the high jump at the 1932 Olympics. She was also a star in basketball, a great baseball player, a skilled bowler, and a fine pool player. Zaharias became most famous as a golfer, winning 41 tournaments between 1940 and 1955.

## OLDEST NHL HOCKEY PLAYER

Imagine playing professional hockey with your sons. Hockey great Gordie Howe did just that and more! Howe holds the title of oldest man to play in the National Hockey League. He tied his skates for his last professional game at age 52. He played 26 seasons in the NHL, and 6 in the World Hockey League.

GORDIE HOWE

## SQUASHING THE COMPETITION

Can you get tired of winning all the time? Just ask Jahangir Khan. The Pakistani squash player holds the record for the longest winning streak by an athlete in a top-level sport. He won an incredible 555 straight matches, but claimed no special training routine except running, playing the game regularly, and drinking two glasses of milk each day.

## HORSE WITH HEART AWARD

Can a horse be considered an athlete? Do they really understand what's going on in a race? It's impossible to say for sure, but Secretariat certainly seemed to love to race and enjoyed the same kind of attention famous athletes often get. Many consider Secretariat to be the greatest thoroughbred racehorse in history. In 1973, he won the Triple Crown—the Kentucky Derby, the Preakness Stakes, and the Belmont Stakes. The Triple Crown is reserved for three-year-old thoroughbreds. The handsome red horse, known for having an abnormally large heart, still holds the record for the fastest time in all three races!

**GAME TIME** ONLY 12 HORSES HAVE EVER WON THE TRIPLE CROWN.

# TOP TOURNEYS

## THERE ARE MANY DIFFERENT
### WAYS TO CROWN A CHAMPION. SOME SPORTS,
such as basketball and hockey, have long play-offs at the end of the season, leading to a single winning team. Professional downhill skiing awards points based on the results of every race during the winter, and adds them up to determine a yearly champion. Tennis has a different tournament every week. In the tennis world, instead of crowning a champion, they keep track of who is ranked number one based on weekly results.

## MASTERS, MAJORS, AND OPENS

Even with tournaments throughout the year, tennis and golf both have special events that carry extra importance for athletes and fans. They're known as Majors or Grand Slam tournaments. In tennis, these are the Australian Open, the French Open, Wimbledon, and the U.S. Open. In golf, there's the Masters, the U.S. Open, the British Open, and the Pro Golf Association Championship.

TIGER WOODS

Professional golfer Tiger Woods was the highest earning sports figure from 2000 to 2010.

SERENA WILLIAMS WITH HER U.S. OPEN TROPHY

**GAME TIME** THE OLDEST ACTIVE SPORTS TROPHY, FROM 1673, IS ARCHERY'S SCORTON SILVER ARROW.

New York Yankees player Derek Jeter hoists the World Series Commissioner's Trophy with teammates after the Yankees defeated the Philadelphia Phillies to win the 2009 Major League Baseball World Series.

**VINCE LOMBARDI TROPHY**

## PLAY-OFF PAYOFF

There's an old saying that "nobody remembers who finishes in second place." That's not always true, but it's usually the champion we remember. Here's a look at the championship round, or the big game of the play-offs, in the major North American team sports.

| Sport | League | Event | Trophy |
|---|---|---|---|
| American Football | National Football League (NFL) | Super Bowl | The Vince Lombardi Trophy |
| Canadian Football | Canadian Football League (CFL) | Grey Cup | The Grey Cup |
| Baseball | American League/ National League | World Series | The Commissioner's Trophy |
| Basketball | National Basketball Association (NBA) | NBA Finals | The Larry O'Brien NBA Championship Trophy |
| Hockey | National Hockey League (NHL) | Stanley Cup Final | The Stanley Cup |
| Soccer | Major League Soccer (MLS) | MLS Cup final | The Philip F. Anschutz Trophy |

# By the Numbers

**5** MLS Cup championships have gone to the Los Angeles Galaxy

**6** Super Bowl titles have been won by the Pittsburgh Steelers

**17** NBA championships have been earned by the Boston Celtics

**24** Stanley Cup titles have been claimed by the Montréal Canadiens

**27** World Series have been won by the New York Yankees

# WHO PLAYS WHAT?

## SOME SPORTS, SUCH AS
### SOCCER, ARE POPULAR ALL OVER THE WORLD.

Others have a huge following, but only in a particular country or region. There are also sports that you would only expect to be popular in certain places that turn up in some pretty interesting spots around the globe.

Alaska (U.S.)

*NORTH*

*AMERICA*

UNITED STATES

**U.S.A.**

It's hard to say for sure who invented snowboarding, but Tom Sims was definitely among the pioneers. In 1963, he built what he called a ski board in the wood shop of his high school in Haddonfield, New Jersey. He wanted to combine his love of skiing and skateboarding. Sims became a world champion in skateboarding and snowboarding.

0 ————— 2,000 miles
0 ————— 2,000 kilometers

**SNOWBOARDING**

## EXPLORER'S CORNER

What other countries call football, people in the United States call soccer. In the United States, football is very different—starting with the fact that players can use their hands to touch the ball, although it is also kicked as in soccer. The National Football League has 32 teams and millions of fans. The sport is spreading in other parts of the world. Currently, there are NFL players who were born in Germany, Canada, Ghana, Poland, and even the small Polynesian island nation of Tonga.

**BRAZIL**

The Formula 1 World Drivers' Championship is awarded each year to the driver who has earned the most points in Grand Prix race results. Brazil is the only South American country to have had three championship drivers: Emerson Fittipaldi, Ayrton Senna, and Nelson Piquet. Formula 1 began crowning a world champion in 1950. Winners have come from many different countries, but mostly from countries in Europe.

BRAZIL

*SOUTH AMERICA*

**FORMULA 1 RACING**

### U.K.

Though we call it soccer in North America, most of the world calls it football. Football (soccer) is extremely popular in England, but American football has its fans there, too. NFL teams began playing games at London's Wembley Stadium in 2007. There are also 70 amateur teams playing American football in leagues across Britain.

Hockey is Canada's favorite sport. It ranks well behind soccer in most European countries, but hockey is also a favorite in Latvia. Latvians are known to plan their vacations around international hockey tournaments; fans cast so many online ballots for the NHL All-Star Game during the 2014-15 season that Latvian player Zemgus Girgensons got more votes than any other player.

### U.A.E.

Dubai is a city of more than two million people in the United Arab Emirates. It lies in the Arabian Desert, where summer temperatures reach 106°F (41.3°C), and winter is still a toasty 75°F (23.9°C). Yet in November of 2005, an indoor ski resort opened with five slopes and a nearby snow park.

### JAPAN

Sumo is a Japanese style of wrestling. It began in ancient times and is still very popular in that country. There are no weight restrictions in Sumo wrestling, so heavier wrestlers have an advantage. The rules are simple: The first wrestler knocked out of the ring or to touch the ground with anything but his feet is the loser.

### ETHIOPIA

Ethiopia is known for its long-distance runners. One of the first and most prominent was Abebe Bikila, who raced to an Olympic gold medal running barefoot through the streets of Rome in 1960. Bikila had always trained in bare feet and chose to race that way, too. He decided to wear running shoes at the Tokyo Olympics in 1964, and he became the first person to win two Olympic marathons.

INDOOR SKI RESORT IN DUBAI

SUMO WRESTLING

ABEBE BIKILA

**GAME TIME** LACROSSE IS A NATIVE AMERICAN GAME WITH MODERN RULES WRITTEN IN 1867.

# A PHOTOGRAPHIC DIAGRAM

## HAVE YOU EVER SEEN A TENNIS

**BALL CHEWED UP BY A DOG? THE "GUTS" OF THE**
ball are a freaky cool mix of a hollow center, and rubber and felt layers. But you don't need canine teeth to see what's inside these sports balls.

### TENNIS BALLS
The International Tennis Federation determines the size of tennis balls. The balls measure about 2.57 to 2.7 inches (6.54 to 6.86 cm) in diameter, and are made of felt-covered rubber. Inside, tennis balls are filled with air. Some are pressurized so they bounce and spin better.

SOCCER BALL

### SOCCER BALLS
According to Fédération Internationale de Football Association (FIFA), the organization that oversees international soccer, a soccer ball must be made of leather or other suitable materials. It must be between 26.7 and 27.5 inches (68 and 70 cm) in circumference and weigh between 14.4 and 16.8 ounces (408 and 476 g). Inside, a soccer ball has a polyester and cotton liner and an air-filled latex bladder.

HOCKEY PUCK

TENNIS BALL

### HOCKEY PUCKS
A hockey puck must be made of vulcanized rubber and must be one inch (2.54 cm) thick and three inches (7.62 cm) in diameter.

## SOFTBALLS

Softball is played with a larger ball than baseball. The yellow optic balls aren't soft at all, and measure 12 inches (30.5 cm) in circumference. Inside, they are stuffed with kapok or cork fiber as well as polyurethane.

## BOWLING BALLS

Ten-pin bowling balls have two or three holes for the ring and middle fingers. They are hefty, and some weigh as much as 16 pounds (7.25 kg). Smooth urethane resin covers the outside of the ball, while the inside is a polyurethane core surrounded by a dense plastic shell.

BOWLING BALL

## BASEBALLS

An official Major League baseball must weigh between 5 and 5.25 ounces (142 and 149 g) and be between 9 and 9.25 inches (22.9 and 23.5 cm) around. The inside of a baseball is made with yarn wound around a small core of cork, rubber, or similar material. Outside, there are two strips of white horsehide or cowhide, stitched tightly together with red thread. There are 108 double stitches holding together the two pieces of leather.

SOFTBALL

## GOLF BALLS

According to the rules of golf, a golf ball can weigh no more than 1.62 ounces (45.93 g). It cannot be less than 1.68 inches (4.267 cm) in diameter. Early golf balls were made of wood, then from leather stuffed with cow hair or feathers from a chicken or goose. These days, most golf balls have a solid rubber or resin core, and a cover made from a different type of rubber. Dimples on a golf ball make it fly farther and have been part of the design since 1905.

GOLF BALL

BASEBALL

Basketball is growing in popularity throughout the world. The National Basketball Association (NBA) now plays global games, or foreign games, in cities such as London, United Kingdom; Shanghai, China; Istanbul, Turkey; and Rio de Janeiro, Brazil.

# 2

# DRIBBLE, DRIVE, HUSTLE

# HOOPS GAME

## VERY FEW SPORTS CAN
### PINPOINT THE EXACT MOMENT WHEN THEY

began. Basketball is one that can. James Naismith introduced the game in 1891 and published the first rules on January 15, 1892. Basketball spread quickly throughout the United States and Canada. It was very popular at high schools and universities. By 1904, basketball was already played in so many countries that it was included at the Olympics as a demonstration sport.

Kids playing basketball in a lot in El Nido, Philippines.

James Naismith invented basketball while working at a YMCA school in Springfield, Massachusetts, in 1891. He was asked to come up with a safe, new sport to be played indoors during winter. He based his original 13 rules for basketball on a stone-throwing game he played as a child and used peach baskets to catch the ball.

## BACK LOT, DRIVEWAY, OR STREET

One of the beauties of basketball is that it's so easy to play—though it's not so easy to play well! All it takes is a ball and a hoop, which can often be found in driveways, school yards, and parks around the world. Players can practice shots by themselves, play one-on-one, or split up into teams of almost any size.

WILT **CHAMBERLAIN** SET AN ALL-TIME NBA SCORING **RECORD** WHEN HE SCORED **100 POINTS** IN A **SINGLE** GAME ON MARCH 2, 1962.

## HEY, HEY, IT'S THE NBA!

Basketball is popular all over the world, and many countries have their own national leagues. However, the National Basketball Association (NBA) in the United States (with one team in Canada) is recognized everywhere as the best in the business. NBA players can make huge salaries, and the arenas are packed for NBA games. The Women's National Basketball Association (WNBA) has teams in some U.S. cities. College basketball in the U.S. is also popular. TV audiences tune in for the annual National Collegiate Athletic Association (NCAA) championships in March and April.

**GAME TIME** THE NBA BEGAN IN 1949 WHEN TWO COMPETING LEAGUES MERGED.

# IN POSITION

Five players from each team are on a court at one time, and each player has a specific position and duties. Just what do they do?

## SHOOTING GUARD

These are often accurate shooters. It is also handy if the shooting guard, or two guard, is a good rebounder.

## SMALL FORWARD

An offensive player who is quick and can hit the basket from the court perimeter

## POWER FORWARD

This big and bulky offense and defense player can catch balls and score.

## CENTER

The tallest player, known as the five. Centers use their size to score and defend.

## POINT GUARD

A good passer and ball handler who "pushes" the ball up the court

# BASKETBALL BASICS

Basketball is a fast-paced game. A lot of action takes place in a short amount of time. Here's a breakdown of a few court basics.

## BASKET

A successful shot is called a basket.

## SLAM DUNK

A slam dunk is when a player jumps above the rim of the basket and slams the ball through.

## DRIVE

To drive in basketball is to run hard toward the net. To dish is to pass the ball.

## COURT

Indoor courts are made of polished wood. The court is rectangular, with a hoop at each end. Courts are divided into two sections by the mid-court line.

## BUZZER BEATER

A last-second shot to win the game is called a buzzer beater.

## MOVING THE BALL

Players move the ball down the court by passing or dribbling. Carrying the ball for more than a step and a half without dribbling is a violation, called traveling.

# TAKE ME OUT TO THE BALL GAME

## BASEBALL IS KNOWN
### AS AMERICA'S NATIONAL PASTIME.

The game has been a favorite in the United States since the middle of the 1800s. It's also very popular in Canada and Japan, as well as in the Caribbean in Puerto Rico, the Dominican Republic, and Cuba.

## IN THE BEGINNING

Nobody really knows who invented baseball. Despite the old stories, it wasn't Abner Doubleday or Alexander Cartwright. Ball-and-bat games may have been played in ancient Egypt and many games with balls and sticks were popular in England hundreds of years ago. The games from England became popular in the United States, too. Modern baseball probably started in New York City in the 1830s. William R. Wheaton wrote the first rules in 1837, and then rewrote them for one of the first organized teams, the New York Knickerbockers, in 1845.

## EXPLORER'S CORNER

Before some Major League Baseball players dreamed of playing in the World Series, they got to play in the Little League World Series in Williamsport, Pennsylvania, U.S.A. Every year, eight teams from the U. S. and eight teams from around the world compete for the championship. In 2014, Mo'ne Davis, who played for a team from Philadelphia, Pennsylvania, became the first female pitcher in Little League World Series history to earn a win and a shutout—she did not give up any runs in the game!

## BIG LEAGUE BASEBALL

The first professional baseball league was the National Association in 1871. It lasted until 1875. In 1876, a new league, called the National League (NL), was formed and still exists today. The American League (AL) began in 1901. Together, these two leagues make up Major League Baseball. Both the NL and the AL had only eight teams when they began. Today, there are 15 teams in each league for a total of 30 big-league ball clubs.

## THE WORLD SERIES

The championship team from the National League began meeting the champion of the American League in the World Series in 1903. The two leagues couldn't come together the following year, but the World Series has been played every season since 1905. Every season but one, that is. The World Series carried on through two World Wars, but it was cancelled in 1994 due to a strike by the players against the team owners.

THE NEW YORK YANKEES IN 1926

## MAJOR LEAGUE HITTING

Some people say that hitting a baseball is the hardest thing to do in sports. The best pitchers can throw the ball more than 100 miles an hour (161 km/h). Only the best hitters in the Major Leagues have a .300 average. That means even they get only three hits in every ten at-bats. The Major League season lasts 162 games, so unlike in other sports, even the best teams know they're going to lose a lot of games.

## BALL UNIFORM

GLOVE

SOCKS

JERSEY

CLEATS

KNEE BREECHES

MOUND

## TALKIN' BASEBALL

Baseball, like all sports, has its own language. Sometimes the language is easy to understand, and sometimes translations are needed:

**AN ACE** is a team's best starting pitcher.

**A BAG** is another name for a base.

**A CAN OF CORN** means an easy catch.

**A DINGER** is a home run.

**A GOPHER BALL** is a pitch hit for a home run.

**A MOON SHOT** is a long, high, deep home run.

**HEAT OR A HEATER** means a good fastball. Sometimes, baseball people will refer to a good fastball as **GOOD CHEESE.**

**FLASHING THE LEATHER** is when a player uses the glove to make a great defensive play.

**TEXAS LEAGUER** is a short hit that drops between an infielder and an outfielder.

**GAME TIME** IN 1947, JACKIE ROBINSON BECAME THE FIRST AFRICAN AMERICAN TO PLAY MAJOR LEAGUE BASEBALL.

# ONE "COOL" GAME

## GLIDING ON SKATES INSTEAD OF RUNNING ON SHOES, HOCKEY PLAYERS CAN MOVE

much faster than the athletes in other team sports, and the sharp blades they wear and the sticks they carry give their sport an extra element of adventure. Although the professional hockey season now stretches well into June, and there are teams in all sorts of warm-weather cities, hockey is still the coolest game on ice.

## ORGANIZED LEAGUES

There are 74 countries that belong to the International Ice Hockey Federation (IIHF). Not all of these countries have their own leagues, but many of them do. Even in Russia, Sweden, Finland, and the Czech Republic, where hockey is very popular, everyone agrees that the top league is the National Hockey League. The NHL had just four teams in its first season of 1917–18, and all of them were in Canada. Today, the NHL has 30 teams, with 23 of them in the United States.

## FROZEN TIME

The true origins of hockey are difficult to trace. Games resembling hockey were played in ancient times, but likely never on ice. Bandy, hurling, and shinty are all games that resemble hockey. They've been popular for hundreds of years in countries such as England, Ireland, and Scotland. Immigrants from those countries brought their games with them to Canada, where cold winters and lots of frozen water meant plenty of places to play the new game of hockey.

**GAME TIME** IN 1924, THE BOSTON BRUINS BECAME THE FIRST AMERICAN TEAM IN THE NHL.

# THE "OTHER" HOCKEY

In North America, it's called field hockey, but to most of the world, it's just called hockey. Field hockey is similar to soccer, only played with a stick and a small plastic ball. There's also an indoor version of the game. Men's teams and women's teams both compete, and there are 130 national associations from all over the world that are members of the International Hockey Federation.

The Stanley Cup is the oldest active trophy in North American team sports. It's even older than the NHL. Canada's governor general, Lord Stanley of Preston, donated the Cup in 1893.

# HOCKEY TALK

**BACK-CHECKING** is when the forwards on a team skate back into their own end to help their defensemen protect the goalie.

To **DANGLE** is to skate all around while carrying the puck, keeping it away from other players and trying to get a shot on goal.

A **POWER PLAY** happens when one team has a player off the ice serving a penalty, giving the other team a one-player advantage.

**STICKHANDLING** is the act of keeping the puck on a player's stick by shifting it quickly from one side of the blade to the other.

The **CREASE** is the area of blue paint directly in front of the goalie net. Nobody is supposed to touch the goalie when the goalie is in the crease.

In the crease, there are five open "holes" the goalie must cover. The **FIVE-HOLE** is right in the middle.

**CREASE**

**CHECKING** includes a number of defensive techniques aimed at keeping an opponent away from the puck.

A **BREAKAWAY** is when the player carrying the puck moves all alone toward the goalie.

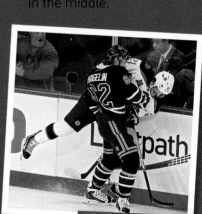

**CHECKING**

**PENALTY**

A **PENALTY** is punishment for rule breaking. Players spend time in a penalty box and their team is shorthanded. The opposing team gets a "power play."

# FOOTBALL, AMERICAN STYLE

## FOR MOST OF THE WORLD, FOOTBALL MEANS SOCCER. BUT AMERICAN FOOTBALL, THE GAME

played with an oval ball on a field with goalposts at each end, is the most popular game in the United States. It's known simply as football.

## DEEP ROOTS

Football evolved from the game of rugby, which itself evolved from soccer. In fact, the first game of football in the United States, played in 1869, was a combination of soccer and rugby. In 1875, Harvard University near Boston, Massachusetts, and McGill University in Montreal, Quebec, played a game that was a slight variation of rugby. Football in both the United States and Canada grew out of that game. People have been paid to play football in the United States since the 1890s, but amateur games at American colleges remained much more popular for many years.

## AN ALL-AMERICAN BALL GAME

The American Professional Football Association began in 1920 and was renamed the National Football League (NFL) in 1922. There have been other leagues besides the NFL over the years, but only the American Football League (AFL) was a real success. The AFL merged with the NFL in 1969. The NFL is split into the National Football Conference (NFC) and the American Football Conference (AFC). Each conference has four divisions (northern, southern, eastern, and western) of 4 teams, for a total of 32 teams. Each conference crowns its own play-off winners who meet to determine the NFL champion in the Super Bowl.

**GAME TIME** GEORGIA TECH BEAT CUMBERLAND 222–0 IN A COLLEGE FOOTBALL GAME ON OCTOBER 7, 1916.

## BIG CROWDS, BIG STADIUMS

With some stadiums holding 91,000 to 100,000 spectators, the National Football League (NFL) has the highest average attendance of any sports league in the world. College football games also draw huge crowds at stadiums all across the United States, as well as on television. Football is also popular with fans in Canada, but the Canadian Football League (CFL) is much smaller than the NFL. The field for Canadian football is bigger than a U.S. football field and each team uses 12 players at a time instead of 11. American football has become popular in Europe, too, with teams and leagues operating in many different countries.

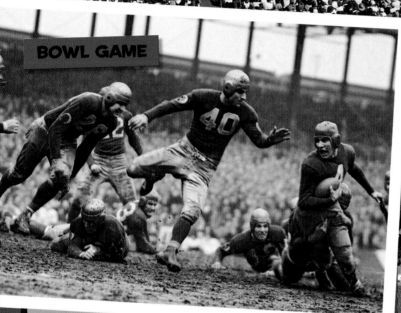

BOWL GAME

The New England Patriots defeated the Seattle Seahawks to win Super Bowl XLIX in 2015.

## THE COLLEGE TRY

College football has many bowl games. The oldest is the Rose Bowl, which is traditionally played on New Year's Day. The Rose Bowl game dates back to 1902. Other major bowl games include the Orange Bowl, the Cotton Bowl, and the Sugar Bowl. The use of the term "bowl" for football games didn't actually begin until 1923, when the Rose Bowl Stadium opened. The bowl name came from the Yale Bowl stadium, which was built in 1913 and was shaped like a big soup bowl.

## BOWLED OVER

Super Bowl Sunday has practically become a national holiday in the United States. Played annually in late January or early February, the big game began in 1967 but wasn't officially called the Super Bowl until 1970. Fans often watch the game at parties, and more than 100 million watch on television. Even people who don't like football tune in to check out the halftime entertainment and special commercials.

# A PHOTO GALLERY

**NICELY DONE!**

## WATCHING
### ATHLETES AT THE TOP OF

their game is thrilling. Whether you attend a professional or Olympic-level sporting event or enjoy them on television—or watch spectacular amateurs in your local park—take notice. It takes a lot of practice, skill, and talent to become a top athlete.

Men and women can compete together in mixed doubles diving.

Rhythmic gymnasts must be strong and flexible.

Pairs skaters skate together for years to develop the trust needed to perform dangerous and delicate lifts.

Short track speed skating is a fast sport in which beginners start young.

In show jumping, horse and rider must work together to pull off clean, or no bars-down, jumps.

Fencing began in Europe as a combat sport in the 1500s.

# A WORLD OF SPORTS

Steeplechase is a sport in which athletes run and jump over obstacles.

# WE ARE THE CHAMPIONS

## THE WORLD OF SPORTS IS CONSTANTLY CHANGING. TEAMS AND PLAYERS

come and go. Rules change, too. What's popular today may not stay that way. For many years, the world's heavyweight boxing champion was the most famous athlete on the planet. Boxing is no longer as popular as it once was, and these days almost every sport you can think of has a way of crowning a world champion. From multi-sport events such as the Olympics to sport-specific events such as World Cup ski racing, there are many ways to crown a champion.

## DON'T BE A DOPE

In a perfect world, the best athletes in any sport would be those who trained the hardest to improve their natural skills. Unfortunately, with so much pressure on athletes to succeed, many of them try to cheat by using anabolic steroids and other performance-enhancing drugs. The first known use of drugs at the Olympics was in 1904, but there were no rules against them then. The IAAF has banned "stimulating substances" since 1928. Today, most sports organizations have drug-testing policies to combat doping.

## ON THE RIGHT TRACK

The International Association of Athletics Federations (IAAF) was established after the 1912 Olympics. It's the world's governing body for track and field (running, jumping, and throwing sports), which is officially known as athletics. The IAAF was created to standardize equipment and competitions and to keep track of world records. The IAAF oversees world championship events in several sports. Many countries also organize their own track-and-field championships for different age levels.

**GAME TIME** THE OFFICIAL DISTANCE OF A MARATHON IS 26 MILES, 385 YARDS (42.195 KM).

# LET THE GAMES BEGIN

The Olympic Games are the best known of the multi-sport games, but there are many other similar sporting events held all over the world. These games are held over several days or weeks, in one "host" city or country. Countries send national teams to the events, and athletes are awarded medals for placing first, second, or third. Here are some of the biggest multi-sport games.

**COMMONWEALTH GAMES:** An Olympics-like sports competition for countries that used to be part of the British Empire. The games are held in the summertime every four years. They began in 1930.

**PAN AMERICAN GAMES:** A competition like the Summer Olympics held for countries in North, Central, and South America. They began in 1951. Only one Winter Pan American Games was held, in 1990.

**X GAMES:** The X stands for "Extreme." These games were created by the television sports network ESPN in 1995 and feature such sports as motocross, mountain biking, and skateboarding.

**WINTER X GAMES:** These began in 1997 and feature snowboarding, snowmobiling, and various types of skiing.

# FASTEST HUMANS ALIVE

Sprinters—especially those running the 100 meters—are popular athletes. The earliest record for running 100 meters was 10.8 seconds, set in 1891. It took until 1968 for the first man to officially run 100 meters in less than 10 seconds. Usain Bolt set the current world record of 9.58 seconds in 2009. The women's world record of 10.49 seconds has stood since 1988.

**USAIN BOLT**

These annual races are among the most famous sporting events in the world.

The Boston Marathon is the oldest annual marathon race. It was first run in 1897, but was inspired by the first modern Olympic marathon in 1896.

The Tour de France is an annual bicycle race through the French and European countryside. It began in 1903. The race has 21 different stages over 23 days.

Races combining running, cycling, and swimming began in France in the 1920s. The first modern triathlon was held in San Diego in 1974. A triathlon is a competition in which athletes swim, cycle, and run in a series of stages. The annual Ironman World Championship has been held in Hawaii since 1978. Competitors swim 2.4 miles (3.9 km), bike ride 112 miles (180.2 km), and then run 26.2 miles (42 km).

# THE OLYMPICS

## EVERY FOUR YEARS, ATHLETES
### FROM ALL OVER THE GLOBE COME TOGETHER FOR
the world's premier sporting event. With Summer Games and Winter Games now held in alternating cycles, there are actually different Olympics held every two years. Athletes in every sport dream of doing their best while representing their country, and there's no greater prize than an Olympic gold medal.

## THE WORLD GATHERS

More than 10,000 athletes from 204 countries competed in 26 different sports at the Summer Olympics in London in 2012. The games were held over 19 days. Two more sports (golf and seven-aside rugby) were added before the 2016 Games in Rio de Janeiro, but all events were scheduled over 17 days. More than 2,800 athletes from 89 countries took part in 15 sports at the 2014 Sochi Winter Olympics. The Winter Olympics lasts 16 days.

The ancient games were depicted on pottery and art.

## OLD AND NEW

The Olympics began in ancient Greece in 776 B.C. They continued for nearly 12 centuries until A.D. 393. Many efforts were made to revive the Olympics in modern times. In 1894, Pierre de Frédy, Baron de Coubertin of France founded the International Olympic Committee (IOC), and the first modern Olympics took place in 1896. They were held in Athens—the capital of Greece. The Winter Olympics was first held in Chamonix, France, in 1924.

## HEAVY METAL

For many athletes, an Olympic medal is the ultimate sports award—but it is a modern Olympics invention. Winners at the ancient Olympics received an olive branch from Mount Olympus. Winners at the first modern Olympics in 1896 received an olive wreath and a silver medal. The gold, silver, and bronze medals for first, second, and third place finishers were introduced at the 1904 St. Louis Olympics. The last time that Olympic gold medals were actually made of gold was 1912. These days, both gold and silver medals contain 92.5 percent silver. There's some copper in them, too.

## ATHLETES OF ABILITY

The Special Olympics is a sports movement for athletes with intellectual disabilities. Founded in 1968, it hosts regional and national competitions as well as the Special Olympics World Games. These are summer and winter games held every four years. Competitors are awarded medals for placing first, second, and third in their events.

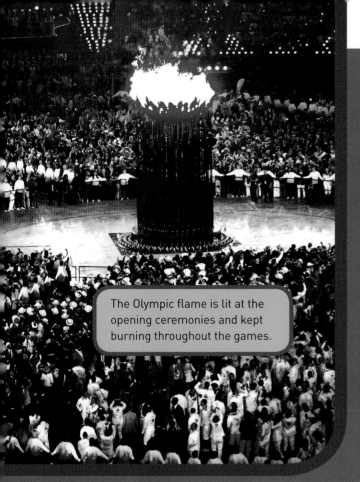

The Olympic flame is lit at the opening ceremonies and kept burning throughout the games.

## A SPORTING CHANCE

Sports such as swimming, gymnastics, athletics, and cycling have been part of the Olympics since 1896. Men's weightlifting also began in 1896, although women have only been allowed to compete in that sport since 2000. Many Olympic sports are popular around the world at all times, but some sports only get attention during Olympics years. Summer sports such as team handball, archery, and rowing, and winter events such as biathlon, don't generate as much interest. When adding new sports to the Olympics, the IOC looks for something with worldwide popularity. Over the years, sports such as croquet, polo, and tug-of-war have been a part of the Olympics. Baseball, lacrosse, and cricket have come and gone from the Summer Olympics over the years.

Paraskiing takes great core body strength.

## EXPLORER'S CORNER

The Summer Olympics are my favorite sporting event. In 1984, gymnast Mary Lou Retton became the first American to win the gold medal for the all-around, with the best total score for the four events. She inspired little girls all over the United States, and the world. Retton was coached by Béla and Márta Károlyi, the same coaches who had trained 1976 all-around gold medalist Nadia Comăneci—and it was Comăneci who had inspired Retton to start doing gymnastics.

## THE PARALYMPIC GAMES

The Paralympics are for athletes with physical disabilities. Like the Olympics, there are Summer Paralympic Games and Winter Paralympics held every four years. Athletes compete in many of the same sports as Olympic competitors and some that have been adjusted for athletes with disabilities, such as wheelchair basketball and sledge hockey. The Summer Paralympics began in 1960 and have been using the same facilities as the Summer Olympics since 1988. The Winter Paralympics began in 1976 and have been sharing Olympic facilities since 1992.

**GAME TIME** SOVIET GYMNAST LARISA LATYNINA WON 14 MEDALS IN INDIVIDUAL EVENTS.

# LIVING ON THE EDGE

## WHAT DO WAKEBOARDING,
### PARKOUR, BASE JUMPING, AND BMX HAVE IN COMMON?

They're all examples of action and adventure sports. The term "extreme sports" gained popularity with the creation of the X Games in the 1990s. But these days, what people think of as extreme or adventure has gone way beyond sports such as skateboarding and paintball. Often what makes an action or adventure sport is the high level of risk or danger involved. Because of that, there aren't a lot of leagues or school competitions in adventure sports. These sports often involve high speeds or high altitudes, so many require specialized equipment.

## CLIMBING THE WALLS

Rock climbing is one action and adventure sport that has become popular. It can be done outdoors on real mountain cliffs, or indoors in special climbing gyms. Basic equipment includes tight-fitting climbing shoes, ropes, and harnesses. Climbers compete in sport climbing competitions, or comps, judged for speed and difficulty. Bouldering and ice climbing are also popular variations of rock climbing. Boulderers climb rock "problems"— studying them to determine sequences of moves that are much like solving puzzles. Unlike rope climbing, boulderers climb without using ropes or harnesses. They use spotters and big mats called crash pads to prevent injuries from falls. Ice climbing is similar to rock climbing, but on frozen waterfalls or cliffs covered in ice. Climbers carry special ice axes in each hand and wear special spikes, called crampons, on their boots.

**GAME TIME** THE EXTREME SPORTS CHANNEL HAS BEEN BROADCASTING EXTREME SPORTS AROUND THE WORLD SINCE 1999.

**38** NGK EVERYTHING

# TO THE EXTREME

**MOUNTAIN BIKING** and **BMX** (bicycle motocross) are now a part of the Summer Olympics, while snowboarding and freestyle skiing are part of the Winter Olympics. Other adventure sports seem more like activities than sports, but all of them are action-packed!

**HANG GLIDING** is a sport in which pilots fly light aircraft that look like big kites. Pilots launch themselves from large hills, and the best hang gliders can remain in the air for hours.

## ULTIMATE FIGHTING

Mixed Martial Arts (MMA) rivals boxing as the world's most popular combat sport. MMA combines the punching elements of boxing with wrestling holds, judo throws, and Brazilian or regular jujitsu. MMA artists cross-train in many different styles, and must learn proper techniques for punches and kicks, as well as holds and takedowns for defending themselves.

## PARKOUR

can be practiced alone or with others. It is about freely moving over any kind of terrain or obstacle to get from one point to another. Parkour can involve running, jumping, climbing, rolling, or whatever is best to get around or over an obstacle.

## WAKEBOARDING

is a combination of waterskiing and snowboarding. It also uses surfing techniques. Wakeboarders are usually pulled by a motorboat such as a ski boat that makes it easy to jump.

# HALL OF FAME

## BASEBALL WAS THE FIRST
**SPORT TO HAVE A HALL OF FAME, INDUCTING**
its first members in 1936. Today, almost every sport has some sort of hall of fame. For many sports, a player has to be retired to be elected. Some halls of fame have minimum victory requirements to gain induction. Most are determined by voting. However an athlete gets there, becoming a member of a sport's hall of fame is the ultimate career accomplishment.

**MICHAEL JORDAN**

**NADIA COMĂNECI**

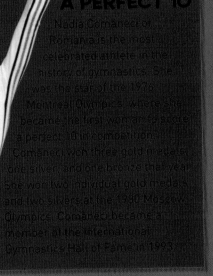

### A PERFECT 10
Nadia Comăneci of Romania is the most celebrated athlete in the history of gymnastics. She was the star of the 1976 Montreal Olympics, where she became the first woman to score a perfect 10 in competition. Comăneci won three gold medals, one silver, and one bronze that year. She won two individual gold medals and two silvers at the 1980 Moscow Olympics. Comăneci became a member of the International Gymnastics Hall of Fame in 1993.

**BABE RUTH**

### AIR JORDAN
Others have scored more points, and some have won more championships, but Michael Jordan may just be the greatest basketball player of all time. Jordan was a ten-time NBA scoring champion, and was also one of the best defensive players in the game. He made all of his teammates better, which helped the Chicago Bulls win six NBA titles in the 1990s. Jordan was elected to the Basketball Hall of Fame in 2009.

### THE SULTAN OF SWAT
Babe Ruth began his career as a star pitcher for the Boston Red Sox in 1914. Later, he became baseball's greatest slugger with the New York Yankees. The single-season record for home runs was 27 before Ruth doubled that with 54 home runs in 1921. When he ended his career in 1935 with 714 home runs, no one else had even hit 500. Ruth was elected to the Baseball Hall of Fame in 1936.

**GAME TIME** MUHAMMAD ALI WAS THE WORLD'S UNDISPUTED HEAVYWEIGHT BOXING CHAMPION THREE TIMES BETWEEN 1964 AND 1979.

## LINDSEY VONN

## STILL THE GREATEST

Though most of his records have been broken, many people still consider Jim Brown to be the greatest football player of all time. Brown played nine seasons with the Cleveland Browns from 1957 to 1965, and won eight rushing titles. He was a Pro Bowl (all-star) running back all nine years, and led the Browns to the NFL Championship in 1964. Brown was selected to the Pro Football Hall of Fame in 1971.

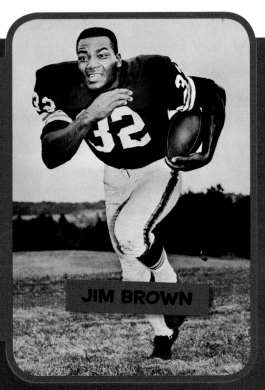

JIM BROWN

## GOING DOWNHILL, FAST

In 2015, American Lindsey Vonn won her 63rd career World Cup race to set a new record for female skiers. Vonn has won the overall World Cup title four times, and the World Cup downhill title every year from 2008 to 2013, and again in 2015. She was the first American woman to win Olympic gold in the downhill event in 2010. Vonn will be eligible for the U.S. Ski and Snowboard Hall of Fame two years after she retires.

# By the Numbers

**3** World Cup titles for Pelé with Brazil are the most won by any soccer player.

**86** World Cup skiing victories is the record set by Sweden's Ingemar Stenmark.

**208** career touchdowns for Jerry Rice is the most in NFL history.

**262** hits by Ichiro Suzuki in 2004 set a single-season Major League Baseball record.

**801** goals by Gordie Howe trail only Wayne Gretzky's 894 in NHL history.

**5,477** passing yards by Peyton Manning in 2013 set the NFL single-season record.

**18,355** rushing yards by Emmitt Smith make him the all-time NFL leader.

**38,387** points were scored by the NBA's all-time leader Kareem Abdul-Jabbar.

## THE GREAT ONE

Wayne Gretzky's incredible vision and skill on the ice made him the NHL's greatest offensive star. Gretzky won seven straight scoring titles in the 1980s, and won the Stanley Cup four times with the Edmonton Oilers. He scored more goals than any other player in hockey history, but was even better at setting up his teammates. Gretzky was elected to the Hockey Hall of Fame in 1999.

WAYNE GRETZKY

# SPORTS COMPARISONS

## YOU VS. THE PROS

## YOU CAN CHEER
**FROM THE SIDELINES OR** join the game and play hard. Many sports have different rules and different fields of play to help "even out the playing field" for young people. That's what makes it different for you vs. the pros.

## FULL-COURT PRESS

In the NBA and NCAA, basketball courts measure 94 feet by 50 feet (28.7 m by 15.2 m). High school basketball courts measure about 84 feet by 50 feet (25.6 m by 15.24 m), and some elementary schools have courts measuring 74 feet by 42 feet (22.5 m by 12.8 m).

## BIG LEAGUE DISTANCES

The distance between the bases in Major League Baseball is 90 feet (27.4 m). In Little League Baseball, players 12 years old and younger usually play on fields with 60 feet (18.2 m) between the bases. All official youth baseball leagues also limit the number of pitches a pitcher is allowed to throw in a game.

# PLAYING TOGETHER

Many organized youth sports leagues are coed, allowing boys and girls to play together until they reach a certain age. There are no coed professional contact sports. But men and women compete with each other on the same level in a variety of other sports, including mixed doubles tennis, mixed doubles curling, equestrian events, pairs skating and ice dancing, and mixed bowling.

# CHECKING UP

Body checking, or using parts of the body to knock an opponent into the boards or onto the ice, is part of professional hockey, but it can lead to injury and concussion for young players. Both Hockey Canada and USA Hockey no longer allow body checking for players playing at the peewee level and lower (anyone under the age of 13).

# TOOLS OF THE TRADE

Everybody has to start somewhere and bicycle racers often start with push-bikes. Push-bikes require young riders to learn to balance without pedals or training wheels. Riders must still wear protective gear such as helmets and sometimes knee pads. Professional bicycle racers ride racing or road bikes that are fast, weigh less than 15 pounds (6.8 kg), and have gear shifters, brake levers, tire chains, and peddles. Professional riders also wear helmets, gloves, special tight-fitting shorts, and cycling shoes that clip into the pedals.

Bicycle motocross, or BMX, is a cycle sport run on dirt tracks. It is also an Olympic sport.

# 4
# SPORTS FUN

# GET IN THE GAME!

## MANY FANS GO CRAZY FOR THEIR SPORTS OR TEAMS.

### THEY BUY T-SHIRTS AND TEAM JERSEYS, AND THEY ATTEND GAMES AND EVENTS

whenever they can. Some fans know everything there is to know about their favorite sport or team, from game stats to pre-game rituals.

HANK AARON
Outfield

BRAVES

Hammerin' Hank Aaron is ranked as one of the 100 greatest baseball players.

A fan asks Chicago White Sox player Scott Radinsky to sign a baseball card.

## PICK A CARD

The first baseball cards were made in the 1860s. They were used by a lot of companies to promote their businesses, even if they had nothing to do with baseball. Later, candy and gum companies became the main producers of baseball and hockey cards. Soon there were cards for almost every major sport. Follow these steps and with a little bit of creativity, you can make your own sports card. Just cut yourself a sports card–size piece of cardboard and get to it.

## MAKE YOUR OWN CARD

PHOTO HERE

2015

FIRSTNAME
LASTNAME

TEAM NAME

3B

COUNTY BASEBALL LEAGUE

**1** Choose a sport, any sport.

**2** Take a picture or draw a picture of you playing that sport or wearing or using that sport's equipment. If you always wanted to be a pole vaulter, here's your chance to be a star. Paste or draw the picture on one side of the cardboard. Put your name, date of birth, and place of birth under your picture.

**3** Write a brief biography of yourself for the other side of the card. There's not a lot of room on the back of a card, but you should write a sentence or two about your best moment in that sport or something funny that happened while playing it. Depending on what sport you choose, you can also list some of your statistics.

# WHAT'S IN A NAME?

Some sports are notorious for athlete nicknames. Nicknames often involve a physical trait, or a special skill that an athlete has, such as the nicknames "Boom Boom" or "Ferocious" for a boxer. If your name is Jimmy or Janie Nelson, and you're good at math, you could be called "Numbers" Nelson. See if you can match the following famous athletes and their descriptions with their nicknames.

**1**

**BOBBY HULL**
hockey (he was blond, swift, and strong)

**2**

**RANDY JOHNSON**
baseball (he was 6 feet 2 inches [188 cm] tall)

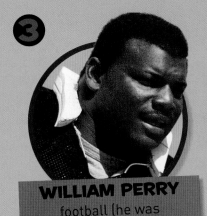

**3**

**WILLIAM PERRY**
football (he was large and wide)

**4**

**JULIUS ERVING**
basketball (he had the skill of a surgeon on the court)

**5**

**MARK FIDRYCH**
baseball (his bushy blond hair made him look like a famous Sesame Street character)

**A** THE BIG UNIT

**B** THE BIRD

**C** THE GOLDEN JET

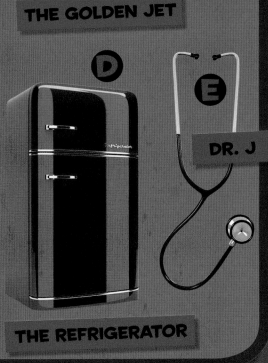

**D** THE REFRIGERATOR

**E** DR. J

---

**GAME TIME** BOB FERGUSON WAS A BASEBALL PLAYER NICKNAMED "DEATH TO FLYING THINGS."

# HEY, REF!

## IN ALMOST EVERY

**SPORTS COMPETITION, THERE'S** a third team taking part. Sometimes, they're right out there on the field, the court, or the ice. Not many people cheer for this team. They're the referees or the umpires. Referees and umpires don't just make sure players follow the rules, they also help keep sports safe. Do you know the rules well enough to make the right call?

**1** It's second down in an NFL game. A receiver is streaking down the sidelines when the quarterback throws the ball. The receiver jumps and catches it. One foot lands inbounds, but the other comes down outside the line. What's the call?

**A.** It's a completion, but the play stops.
**B.** It's an incomplete pass.
**C.** Pass interference
**D.** Repeat second down

**2** The losing hockey team has pulled its goalie. A player takes a shot at the empty net. It's going in, but someone from the other team throws their stick and knocks the puck away. What's the call?

**A.** two-minute penalty
**B.** five-minute penalty
**C.** penalty shot
**D.** awarded goal

**3** There's a runner on first base. The batter hits the ball. Before anyone can get a glove on it, the ball hits the base runner. What's the call?

**A.** The runner is out.
**B.** The batter is out.
**C.** The ball is dead; the batter and runner each get one base.
**D.** The ball is live; everyone can keep running until someone makes a play.

## CHECK YOUR SCORE

Even if you don't want to be a referee, it's important to know the rules of the games you play. How did you do?

**1 = B**  In the NFL, a receiver must have both feet in bounds for a catch to count. In college football and the Canadian Football League, only one foot has to be in bounds.

**2 = D**  Normally, if a player or goalie throws their stick at the puck, the result is a penalty shot. If the net is empty at the time, the player who shot the puck is awarded a goal.

**3 = A**  Baseball rules say that a runner who gets hit by the ball is out ... unless the ball was touched by a fielder first. Any other runners have to go back to their base.

**4 = A**  Officials may award touches to the opponent if a fencer attacks with both hands.

**5 = C**  Arrows that pierce the lines between the circles are awarded the points from the higher-scoring circle.

**6 = B**  Two points are deducted from a skater's score for any illegal element or movement, and somersault jumps are illegal.

## DID YOU MAKE THE RIGHT CALL?

### IF YOU SCORED 4–6
You could be a referee, or a coach ... or the captain of your team!

### IF YOU SCORED 2–3
You're still a star player, but you might want to study up on the rules.

### IF YOU SCORED 0–1
You're a fine player, but don't argue with the referee!

---

**4** In fencing, competitors score a single point each time they touch their opponent's body with their weapon. If one touches the opponent while holding their weapon with both hands, what does the official do?

A. Attacking with two hands is illegal; the official can award a touch to the opponent.
B. Attacking with two hands is legal and the attacker scores a point.
C. Action is halted and restarted with no points awarded.
D. The two-handed attacker is disqualified from the match.

**5** A target in archery features circles surrounding a bull's-eye in the middle. In the Olympics, a bull's-eye scores 10 points. If an arrow strikes the target directly on a line between two circles, what is the result?

A. The archer fires again.
B. The shot counts for the lower score.
C. The shot counts for the higher score.
D. The shot counts for zero points.

**6** Certain lifts, spins, and jumps in figure skating are considered illegal. If a skater performs a somersault type of jump, what is the ruling from the judges?

A. The skater is disqualified.
B. Two points are deducted.
C. Ten points are deducted.
D. Somersaults are legal.

**GAME TIME**  TEN OF THE 310 MEMBERS OF THE BASEBALL HALL OF FAME ARE UMPIRES.

# TOOLS OF THE TRADE

## HEY, WHAT'S THAT THINGAMABOB?

**WHAT SPORT DOES IT BELONG TO? ALL SPORTS FOLLOW** rules, and many use specific equipment and techniques. Can you match the question to the equipment, rule, or technique shown in the images?

**①** LIKE KNIGHTS OF OLD, THESE ARE WORN TO PROTECT THE FACE AND NECK AGAINST INJURIES IN WHICH SPORT?
.............................................

**②** THE SPORT THAT USES THIS OBJECT HAS BEEN AROUND SINCE ANCIENT TIMES. WHAT IS IT?
.............................................

**③** THOUGH HE (OR SHE) APPEARS TO BE FACING THE WRONG WAY, THIS PERSON IS RESPONSIBLE FOR STEERING THE BOAT AND SHOUTING OUT COMMANDS TO THE ROWERS.
.............................................

**④** IN GYMNASTICS, THERE ARE TRADITIONAL TYPES OF EQUIPMENT, AND COMPETITIONS FOR MEN AND WOMEN. WHAT ARE THE TWO PIECES OF EQUIPMENT SHOWN HERE, AND WHO COMPETES ON WHICH ONE?
.............................................

**⑤** SKELETON RACING IS LIKE A HEAD-FIRST TOBOGGAN RIDE. WHAT DO SKELETON RACERS USE AS BRAKES?
.............................................

**⑥** WHAT'S THE NAME OF THIS SPORT THAT COMBINES CROSS-COUNTRY SKIING WITH SHOOTING A RIFLE?

**Ⓐ**

### Ⓑ NO BRAKES!
There are no brakes! Competitors who try to slow down on the course are disqualified. At the end of the race, athletes stop their sleds by using their feet. There are no brakes on a luge either.

**GAME TIME** THE JAMAICAN BOBSLED TEAM FIRST COMPETED AT THE WINTER OLYMPICS IN CALGARY IN 1988.

POMMEL HORSE

**C**

## BALANCE BEAM AND POMMEL HORSE

A balance beam is used by female gymnasts. The beam stands just over 4 feet (1.2 m) above the floor. It's 16 feet (4.9 m) long, but only 3.9 inches (9.9 cm) wide. A pommel horse is used by male gymnasts. It was originally developed centuries ago as an artificial horse for soldiers to practice mounting and dismounting.

**D**

## BIATHLON

The word comes from a Greek word meaning "two contests." (A triathlon combines three contests: running, swimming, and cycling.) Similar events date back to the 1700s, but the first modern biathlon was probably organized by Norway's army in 1912.

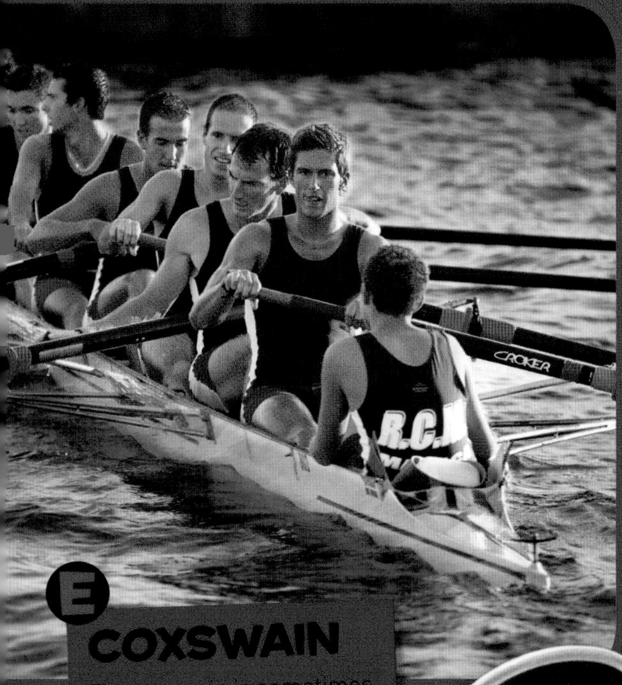

**E**

## COXSWAIN

The coxswain is sometimes shortened to cox. The literal meaning of this term is "boat servant" and the main job of this person is to keep the boat and rowers safe. At the end of a competition, the rowers in the winning boat will traditionally throw their coxswain into the water.

**F**

## DISCUS

The piece of equipment is called a discus. The sport is officially known as discus throw. In the men's competition, the discus weighs 4.4 pounds (2 kg) and is 8.6 inches (21.9 cm) in diameter. A women's discus is 3.9 pounds (1.7 kg) and 7.1 inches (18 cm) in diameter.

# FACT VS. MYTH

## SPORTS ARE FULL
### OF LEGENDARY PERFORMERS AND

performances, but not all of the tales are true. Do you know which of these stories are fact and which are myth?

**A** FOOTBALLS ARE NICKNAMED "PIGSKINS" BECAUSE THEY ARE MADE FROM THE SKIN OF PIGS.

**B** THROWING SPITBALLS HAS ALWAYS BEEN AGAINST THE RULES IN MAJOR LEAGUE BASEBALL.

**C** SLAM DUNKS ARE HUGELY POPULAR IN BASKETBALL, BUT DUNKING WAS ONCE AGAINST THE RULES IN COLLEGE BASKETBALL.

**D** WHEN THE MODERN OLYMPICS BEGAN IN 1896, WOMEN WERE NOT ALLOWED TO COMPETE.

**E** EVEN THOUGH FANS OFTEN THROW HATS ON THE ICE WHEN A HOCKEY PLAYER SCORES THREE GOALS IN A GAME, THE TERM "HAT TRICK" WAS NOT INVENTED FOR HOCKEY.

## A. MYTH
Early balls were often made from the bladders of animals, including pigs. Later, they were covered with leather, which helped popularize the term "pigskin" for footballs. Today, many footballs are made from vulcanized rubber, but official balls for league play are made of leather, which comes from cattle.

## B. MYTH
These days, pitchers have to ask permission just to blow on their hands to keep them warm in cold weather. In the early days, pitchers could lick their fingers to get a better grip, and some would actually spit into their hand or lick the ball! Putting anything on a baseball can change its spin and make it move unpredictably, so baseball banned spitballs in 1920.

**GAME TIME** FORWARD PASSES WERE FIRST ALLOWED IN AMERICAN FOOTBALL IN 1906 BUT NOT UNTIL 1929 IN CANADA.

American track star Wilma Rudolph was considered the fastest woman in the world in the 1956 and 1960 Olympic Games.

## C. FACT

Bob Kurland was 7 feet [2.1 m] tall when he played college basketball for Oklahoma State and led the United States to Olympic gold medals in 1948 and 1952. He was the first player to dunk the ball regularly. However, the NCAA banned dunking between 1967 and 1976.

## D. FACT

No women competed at the Olympics in 1896, and in 1900 only 22 of the 997 athletes were women. Women were not allowed to compete in athletics events at the Olympics until 1928.

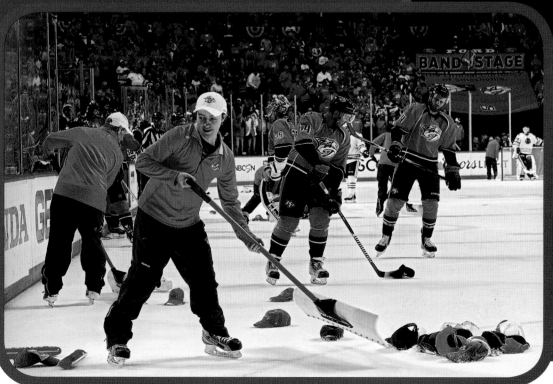

## E. FACT

The term "hat trick" actually comes from the English game of cricket. It originally referred to a bowler who takes three wickets with three straight balls, which is sort of like a pitcher in baseball striking out three straight batters. The term is most popular in hockey, but doing three of almost anything in sports is often referred to as a hat trick.

# PHOTO FINISH

## SPORTS HAVE BEEN A BIG PART OF MY LIFE
### FOR A VERY LONG TIME, FIRST AS A COMPETITIVE ATHLETE AND NOW AS

a reporter covering events. In a funny way, my worst moment as an athlete was also the jumping-off point for my career. In high school, I loved doing track and field—the hurdles in particular. At the Rhode Island State Championships my junior year, when I was ready to show I was the best hurdler in the state, I fell over the first hurdle and could not finish the race. I cried that day. I was upset with myself. It was the first time I had ever fallen in a race, and it happened in the biggest race of my life!

A few months later, I began an internship at the *Providence Journal* newspaper. I wrote about that race, the pain of falling, and my embarrassment. The sports editor put my story on the cover of the sports section and then asked me if I wanted to learn how to become a sports writer. I gladly said yes.

That's one of the great things about sports: They can be a great teacher. Sports should be fun first and foremost, but as athletes push themselves and compete, they will succeed, but sometimes they will fail. And how you deal with both wins and losses can help you become the best possible person you can be.

On February 1, 2015, I was at Super Bowl XLIX in Arizona and watched Patriots player Malcolm Butler give up a very tough catch to Seattle wide receiver Jermaine Kearse, a catch that put Seattle in position to take the lead and possibly win the championship. Butler was very upset with himself on the sideline, and his teammates did their best to encourage him. Two plays later, Butler used what he had learned in practice, predicted the play Seattle wanted to run, and made an interception, clinching the win for New England. Just as one of my worst sports moments led to something great, Butler was able to bounce back and make a fantastic play, a play that made him a hero. And it was my job to write about it!

Shalise competing in an indoor 45-meter hurdle event in her junior year when she was 16. She began hurdling in high school.

New England Patriots cornerback Malcolm Butler with the goal-line interception in Super Bowl XLIX that secured the championship

# AFTERWORD

## DO SPORTS REALLY MATTER? THE ANSWER TO THAT QUESTION IS YES, AND FOR SO MANY

reasons. Sports (and play) can sure make our lives better in a lot of little ways, and some big ones too. The exercise we get by playing sports is good for our bodies and our minds, and the lessons we learn about dedication, teamwork, and sportsmanship are good for building character. Sports can mirror the world we live in too—and be a model for how we want it to be. Take for instance athletes such as Olympic runner Jesse Owens, boxer Joe Louis, and baseball player Jackie Robinson. They were trailblazers in an era when African Americans were not allowed to train, travel, or compete in professional sports on an equal level. Their legendary accomplishments helped open up people's eyes to the issue of civil rights. Female athletes are constantly at the forefront of equality in sports. Women fought to be included in the modern Olympic Games and continue to push for equality in amateur and professional sports competitions and leagues.

Many people take sports very seriously, but even for pros they're also supposed to be fun. Few other things can bring thousands of people together in one place—or cause millions (and even billions!) to tune in on television just to cheer. Going to a game with your family or friends, whether in a big stadium or at a local park or arena, can be a great bonding experience. So, too, can playing catch, or shooting baskets.

### BREAKING BARRIERS IN SPORT

Baseball player Jackie Robinson changed the game forever when in 1947 he joined the Brooklyn Dodgers and became the first African American to play Major League Baseball. Robinson was a legend on and off the field. He was voted Rookie of the Year in 1947, and National League Player of the Year in 1949, despite facing prejudice. Robinson became a pioneer of civil rights and was admired not just for his skill and achievements in baseball, but also for his determination to live with dignity and change the world he lived in. Other athletes followed in Robinson's footsteps: Althea Gibson became the first black tennis player to play in a U.S. National Championship tournament in 1950. She went on to win 11 Grand Slam titles. Manon Rhéaume was the first woman to play exhibition games on an NHL team in 1992. Today, many athletes fight for gender and pay equality in sports and also in their lives outside of sports.

Jackie Robinson greeting fans at a Brooklyn Dodgers game

Sportsmanship is just one of the important lessons of sports.

Joe Louis and Jesse Owens were groundbreakers in sports and in life.

Surfing is a sport that originated in Polynesia. Surfers ride the waves for fun and competition. The International Surfing Association (ISA) World Surfing Games is a yearly event that features team and individual competitions.

# AN INTERACTIVE GLOSSARY

## SPORTS LINGO

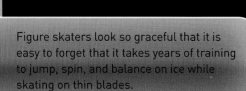

Figure skaters look so graceful that it is easy to forget that it takes years of training to jump, spin, and balance on ice while skating on thin blades.

# THE BALL IS IN YOUR COURT. ARE YOU READY TO

## CRUSH THE COMPETITION WITH A TEST OF YOUR SPORTS SMARTS? START HERE

with this glossary of words and meanings, and check the pages listed. The answers are at the bottom of the page!

## 1. Amateur

A person who plays a sport without being paid
(PAGES 7, 17, 28, 30, 56)

**Which of these major sports organizations is for amateur athletes?**

a. the National Basketball Association
b. the National Collegiate Athletic Association
c. the National Football League
d. the National Hockey League

## 2. Annual

Something which takes place every year
(PAGES 12, 22, 29, 35)

**Which of these is not an annual sports event?**

a. the Boston Marathon
b. the Pan American Games
c. the Tour de France
d. Wimbledon

## 3. Championship

A contest to determine a winner, often involving a series of games or matches
(PAGES 5, 12, 14, 15, 16, 22, 24, 34, 35, 40, 41)

**What is the name of the National Hockey League championship trophy?**

a. The Canada Cup
b. The Grey Cup
c. The Commissioner's Trophy
d. The Stanley Cup

## 4. Civil rights

The rights of all people in a country to be treated equally under the law
(PAGE 56)

**Which of these men was a baseball player and civil rights champion?**

a. Jesse Owens
b. Muhammad Ali
c. Jackie Robinson
d. Joe Louis

## 5. Conference

A group of teams that play against each other, usually within a larger league (PAGE 28)

**What are the names of the divisions that play within each of the National Football Conference (NFC) and American Football Conference (AFC) in the NFL?**

a. Northern and Southern
b. Halas, Lambeau, Mara, Rooney
c. National and American
d. Summer and Fall

## 6. Federation

An organization within which smaller leagues or associations are members (PAGES 11, 18, 26, 27, 34)

**The International Association of Athletics Federations was organized in 1912 as the governing body for which sports?**

a. all sports
b. the Olympics
c. athletics
d. the World Cup

## 7. Grand Prix

A major sporting competition, race, or set of races for many sports, including skating, athletics, and Formula 1 auto racing (PAGE 16)

**Which South American country has produced three championship Formula 1 drivers?**

a. Argentina
b. Venezuela
c. Brazil
d. Bolivia

## 8. League

A collection of sports teams that play against each other over a period of time to win a championship (PAGES 12, 13, 15, 16, 17, 19, 22, 24-25, 26, 28-29, 38, 41, 42-43, 49, 52, 56)

**What was the name of the first professional baseball league?**

a. the American League
b. the American Association
c. the National Association
d. the National League

## 9. Polyurethane

A rubberlike plastic used to give materials a tough outer coating
(PAGE 19)

**Which two sports equipment items are made with polyurethane?**

a. bowling balls
b. footballs
c. softballs
d. basketballs

## 10. Professional

A person who is paid for playing a sport
(PAGES 7, 13, 14, 24, 26, 28, 30, 43, 56)

**Which professional sports league began in 1920 as the American Professional Football Association?**

a. Major League Soccer
b. the All-American Football Conference
c. the American Football League
d. the National Football League

## 11. Thoroughbred

A breed of horses known for their speed and agility in horseracing
(PAGE 13)

**Which of these races is not part of American horse racing's Triple Crown?**

a. the Breeder's Stakes
b. the Belmont Stakes
c. the Kentucky Derby
d. the Preakness Stakes

**ANSWERS: 1.** b; **2.** b; **3.** d; **4.** c; **5.** a and c; **6.** c; **7.** b; **8.** c; **9.** a and c; **10.** d; **11.** a

# FIND OUT MORE

Love sports and want to get further into the game? Try these resources to learn more about sports.

## SPORTS WEBSITES

**Kids: Ask your parents for permission to search online.**

mlb.com/home • nhl.com

nba.com • nfl.com

The official sites of Major League Baseball, the National Basketball Association, the National Football League, and the National Hockey League provide information on the leagues, the sports, players, and current rules and regulations.

**bestkidswebsites.com/category/sports**
A website compiling all sorts of sports sites that will encourage you to put down your electronic gadgets and be more active.

**learn4good.com/games/sports.htm**
Sports games for free to play on your PC, Mac, or iPad, with no download.

**mascothalloffame.com**
A website dedicated to sports mascots with an actual museum set to open in Whiting, Indiana, in 2017.

## PLACES TO VISIT

**The Olympic Museum**
Lausanne, Switzerland

**Skateboarding Hall of Fame and Museum**
Simi Valley, California

## OUT-OF-THIS-WORLD BOOKS

*Babe Didrikson Zaharias: The Making of a Champion*
By Russell Freedman
HMH Books for Young Readers, 2014.

*The Big Book of Hockey for Kids*
By Eric Zweig
Scholastic Canada, 2013.

*Everything Soccer*
By Blake Hoena
National Geographic Kids, 2014.

**NG Staff for This Book**
Shelby Alinsky, *Project Editor*
James Hiscott, Jr., *Art Director*
Jeff Heimsath, *Photo Editor*
Debbie Gibbons, *Director of Intracompany Cartography*
Mike McNey, *Map Research and Production*
Paige Towler, *Editorial Assistant*
Sanjida Rashid and Rachel Kenny, *Design Production Assistants*
Tammi Colleary-Loach, *Rights Clearance Manager*
Mari Robinson and Michael Cassady, *Rights Clearance Specialists*
Kathryn Williams, *Special Projects Assistant*
Grace Hill, *Managing Editor*
Joan Gossett, *Senior Production Editor*
Lewis R. Bassford, *Production Manager*
Rachel Faulise, *Manager, Production Services*
Susan Borke, *Legal and Business Affairs*
Jasmine Lee, *Imaging*

**Published by the National Geographic Society**
Gary E. Knell, *President and CEO*
John M. Fahey, *Chairman of the Board*
Melina Gerosa Bellows, *Chief Education Officer*
Declan Moore, *Chief Media Officer*
Hector Sierra, *Senior Vice President and General Manager,
    Book Division*

**Senior Management Team, Kids Publishing and Media**
Nancy Laties Feresten, *Senior Vice President*
Erica Green, *Vice President, Editorial Director, Kids Books*
Jennifer Emmett, *Vice President, Content*
Eva Absher-Schantz, *Vice President, Visual Identity*
Rachel Buchholz, *Editor and Vice President,* NG Kids *magazine*
Jay Sumner, *Photo Director*
Amanda Larsen, *Design Director, Kids Books*
Hannah August, *Marketing Director*
R. Gary Colbert, *Production Director*

**Digital**
Laura Goetzel, *Manager*
Sara Zeglin, *Senior Producer*
Bianca Bowman, *Assistant Producer*
Natalie Jones, *Senior Product Manager*

**Editorial, Design, and Production by
    Plan B Book Packagers**

**Captions**
Cover: All sports require physical skill and agility and mental
    toughness. To compete professionally, or at elite levels such as at
    the Olympic Games, athletes must spend years training their minds
    and their bodies.
Page 1: Swimming is one of the most popular sports in competitions
    and the Olympics.
Pages 2–3: The fastest hurdlers usually run three large strides between
    each hurdle. Hurdlers must maintain their speed and stride length
    throughout a race or they may hit their hurdle and knock it over.

The National Geographic Society is one of the world's
largest nonprofit scientific and educational organizations.
Founded in 1888 to "increase and diffuse geographic
knowledge," the Society's mission is to inspire people to
care about the planet. It reaches more than 400 million
people worldwide each month through its official journal,
*National Geographic,* and other magazines; National
Geographic Channel; television documentaries; music;
radio; films; books; DVDs; maps; exhibitions; live events;
school publishing programs; interactive media; and
merchandise. National Geographic has funded more than
10,000 scientific research, conservation, and exploration
projects and supports an education program promoting
geographic literacy.

For more information, please visit
nationalgeographic.com, call 1-800-NGS LINE (647-5463),
or write to the following address:
National Geographic Society
1145 17th Street N.W.
Washington, D.C. 20036-4688 U.S.A.

Visit us online at nationalgeographic.com/books

For librarians and teachers: ngchildrensbooks.org

More for kids from National Geographic:
kids.nationalgeographic.com

For information about special discounts for bulk purchases,
please contact National Geographic Books Special Sales:
ngspecsales@ngs.org

For rights or permissions inquiries, please contact
National Geographic Books Subsidiary Rights:
ngbookrights@ngs.org

Paperback ISBN: 978-1-4263-2333-1
Reinforced library binding ISBN: 978-1-4263-2334-8

Printed in Hong Kong
15/THK/1